**HOW TO CREATE
AN UNFORGETTABLE GIFT**

## A HIGH SCHOOL GRADUATION BOOK

**Gordon Burgett**

---

A lifelong keepsake that captures an event,
memory, and one-time rite of passage
forever in print in words and photos

**How to Create an Unforgettable Gift, a High School Graduation Book**. Printed in the United States of America. Copyright © 2011 by Communication Unlimited. All rights reserved. No part of this book may be used or reproduced in any manner whatsoever without written permission except in the case of brief quotations embodied in critical articles and reviews.

For information, contact
Communication Unlimited
P.O. Box 845, Novato, CA 94948
(800) 563-1454 www.gordonburgett.com

First printing, July 2011

▶ Cover Design by Laura Shinn
▶ Proofreading by Linda Lange

ISBN 9780982663547 (Bound)
ISBN 9780982663554 (Digital)

---

The purpose of this manual is to educate and entertain. The author and Communication Unlimited shall have neither liability nor responsibility to any person or entity with respect to any loss or damage caused, or alleged to be caused, directly or indirectly by the information contained in this book. *If you do not wish to be bound by the above, you may return the book, with a purchase receipt, to the publisher for a full refund.*

---

How to Create an Unforgettable Gift:
**A High School Graduation Book**

# Table of Contents

Introduction, 5

| | | |
|---|---|---|
| **1.** | A quick summary: from the idea to the printed pages! | 9 |
| **2.** | What must you do first to give your book form and content? | 15 |
| **3.** | Must you do it alone? | 21 |
| **4.** | A checklist and a timetable are invaluable… | 25 |
| **5.** | Finding the right words to create a fun masterpiece | 37 |
| **6.** | Do you need anybody's permission? | 49 |
| **7.** | A collective venture? | 55 |
| **8.** | Picking the best free publisher | 59 |
| **9.** | Inserting the photos to match the text | 65 |
| **10.** | Creating a fast, free cover | 77 |
| **11.** | Submitting the book to the publisher | 91 |

| | | |
|---|---|---|
| **12.** | Telling others that the book exists | 111 |
| **13.** | Earning book royalties too | 119 |
| **14.** | Why stop with a graduation book? | 121 |

**Special Pages:**

| | |
|---|---|
| The Most Important Steps | 19 |
| Sample Book Text | 35 |
| How the Printed Text Looks | 54 |
| Copyright | 58 |
| Definition of "High School" | 108 |
| Possible Additional Costs | 109 |
| Sample Layout Page | 117 |
| E-book? Bound book? Or both? | 125 |
| Resources | 127 |

Index, 129
Order Form, 131

# Introduction

Almost all of us in the United States honor certain capstone events in our lives. Birth, of course (or the rest makes no sense), maybe baptism, high school graduation, marriage, divorce (say some of the ex-married), and death.

Yet none of them seems to linger longer in the memory than high school graduation, probably because it happens just once and takes place at a critical junction in our development.

Do you have a teen (or even a tyke) who will graduate from high school in the near (or far) future? Then why not create a gift for them that they will never forget, lose, or sell—their own high school graduation book!

It won't be like their school yearbook, if their school has one. That's a super memento but it is published for the entire class. Of course your child will appear in it, as will friends, the homeroom class, team photos, and scattered shots of the campus, prom, and key events.

I'm proposing a book (bound or an e-book, or both) with only one star—your child! It will be about his or her graduation, captured in print and photos so it can be remembered just as it was, forever. The cast will include friends, family, pet(s), sweetheart, and memories.

The author will be you.

And the publisher will be one of the seven or so "ancillary publishers" that understands the publishing so you don't have to. All you must send them is the text, the digital photos, and a cover.

Don't worry, it's easy, fast, and almost free!

Better yet, you can have this book produced once, 12 times, or as many thousands of times as there are folks eager to buy it.

1000 times? Sound nuts? But what if your offspring becomes famous? How many people would buy an original Elvis graduation book if it were readily available today? If that happens, you will even earn a fat royalty from every book sold! (Isn't it about time you cashed in on the kid?)

The cost of this book is almost as miraculous as the thought of your child paying you back with royalties! To publish the book and even to sell it worldwide won't cost you a dime. (A slight exaggeration: it will cost you the shipping of the first bound copy back for you to proof. Figure $10-25.)

The digital version is totally free and available within an hour or two after you accept its proof at the website. The bound version takes about 10 days to arrive, after you give your blessing to the proof, plus a few more days to be publicly salable.

How all of that is done is what I will share with you on the pages that follow.

Incidentally, I'm not involved in this publishing process, other than to share the idea and most of the how-to steps on these pages. It's your book to create.

Why do it? Because it can be the very best kind of one-on-one personal gift you could give to your graduate—unforgettable, kept a lifetime, shared with your grandkids, and their grandkids... You can also have lots of copies made to give to the grandparents, uncles and aunts, family friends, anybody who loves you and the graduate and will treasure such a memory keepsake.

Eager to know more?

You probably have two dozen—or 200—questions to ask. Since I don't know which questions you'd choose, let me give you several hundred answers as I outline a how-to, step-by-step process that (with patience) will give you far more than enough material to build your own, unique gift.

Chapter 1

# A quick summary: from the idea to the printed pages!

Eager to get going on your high school graduation book? Super!

As I'll explain in a subsequent chapter, you needn't do it alone. You might get your other kids involved, your mate, your parent or parents, even the graduate—if it's not to be a surprise. (Or a group of other like-intended parents...) More on that later.

For now, more important is what you might put in the book.

What kind of information, writing, and photos would fill your gift with meaning and fun?

The lists below offer some suggestions. I'll elaborate on most of them as we go along. But if I leave something out or put too much in, don't fret. It's your book, you decide what needs beefing up, omitting, or creating whole-hog. You are the author—it's about your graduate!

Who's the star? Yep, you need a section about

**The graduate**
Their life before high school graduation
Where they lived
Most memorable things they did
Local places they most frequented
Schools they attended
The other kids they grew up with
Pets, bikes, a car, special awards
Skills they developed
Things they most want to remember

Most graduates have families and friends, so two more sections might be

**Their family**
Their folks
Their grandfolks (and great grandfolks)
Brothers and sisters
Aunts, uncles, cousins, other close kin

**Their cronies, cohorts, and collaborators**
Lifelong friends
Boyfriends/girlfriends

Bullies and foes
Other buddies

Some graduates are social gadflies, others are barely popping out of their social cocoons, so sections about this part of their lives must usually be done with particular discretion:

**Their social life**
Parties and big events when they were younger
High school parties, proms, and fun times
Special events, trips, or activities
Summer fun

**Their activities**
What they enjoyed doing before high school
High school sports and clubs
Jobs they had before and during high school
Church, Scouts, outdoor doings...

The only thing that can't be forgotten is the graduation itself!

**The Graduation**
Senior year calendar of graduation events
Cap-gown selection
Pre-ceremony preparation
Graduation program
Post-ceremony activity
Special guests
Special gifts, guidance, and assistance
What the graduate wants to remember forever

You may want to include more special sections too, particularly for those who are heading to college, the military, or training. Want to inject some sage (or dumb) advice, some ribbing, or a perhaps some testimonials in this life-kept book?

**Future Hopes**
Plans for the coming year
Thoughts about the next 5-10 years
A general plan for life

**Testimonials**
From the family
From friends

Or you might want to add something more that can't be contained within a book's covers. Perhaps a repository of physical things about or belonging to the graduate that you have gathered up. A kind of treasure chest—a box, really. You may wish to refer to it (or explain it) in your book.

**A Treasure Chest**
What's in the repository?
Where is it currently stored?

You'll want your graduation gift book to look professional too, so it isn't just dismissed as something hastily thrown together and printed at the town copy shop. Why? Because you want your graduate to show it proudly to friends rather than hiding it in a drawer because it's embarrassing. And because it comes from you, is special, and because it can or will be an extended offering to kin and friends about the big event.

Anyway, the publishers will print a bookstore-quality bound book (or e-book), so you want to keep the contents and photos at that same level.

Finally, the photos. You don't need hundreds and they needn't be studio shots. But you may want 15-50 and (except where they are vintage prints) you'll want clear digital shots saved in .jpg format. (Don't panic: .jpg is how your point-and-push digital camera photos are produced.)

The photos are the fun part, so relax. Building a high school graduation book is like baking that party cake: not too many ingredients, all folded in on schedule, a bit of fancy covering, and the right amount of cooking in the publisher's oven. Out pops a dandy book, with a dozen or 1,000 copies. (Remember Elvis.)

## Chapter 2

## What you must do first to give your book form and content

Mostly, plan. In Chapter 4 we will make lists, then convert those lists into a spiffy book that any graduate (well, most graduates) would gloat about.

A starting point: **do you really want to do this?** It will take some work, a few bucks, and a bit of lost sleep wondering if it's as great an idea as it sounds, if it will look OK, and if others will think you a bit too proud for preserving the graduation almost forever.

So let's address each of those, sort of in reverse order.

Who cares what others think about you wanting you to create and give your kid something unforgettable and invaluable? How often do you get that chance (other than every day)? It's really none of their business. So that's that.

The money. If you have a camera and computer, or can borrow and use them, you're set. You don't need special camera attachments or any more or different software than almost all computers already have. Two of the possible graduation book publishers will let you use their software free to design a decent cover—although if you want some knock-out fancy cover, you can either get a kid to do it, probably free, or you might pay $50-100 (or more). And there is that shipping fee to get the bound book proof back, but $25 should cover that.

As for work, yes, somebody has to design or at least plan the contents, get the facts, take or finagle the photos (more later), put it all together, pick the publisher(s), perhaps design the cover, submit the files, proof the masterpiece, and wrap the package. But we are talking odd hours now and then, not a season or a lifetime.

And yes you will loose some zzzs and wonder if it will look as good as you plan. What's new?

So, if you decide it's a go, then another key question is whether it will be a secret. Will you prepare this book clandestinely, hiding the tools, the layouts, and your plans in your bedroom bloomer drawer? Or will the graduate be told about your coming gift so you can get valuable information from him in a timely fashion? (Our lucky grad book recipient here is Ben, a boy. There is no structural or process difference if it's a Benita, a girl.)

The secrecy issue is particularly important because there will be a necessary time lag between the actual graduation ceremony and party and the book's appearance—mostly to get the ceremony photos included. So if you don't tell the person what's up, how will you explain your gift's absence when others are gifting?

And if you do tell, do you ask the grad if he would like the book as a gift from you? If your heart is in it but he says no or is indifferent, what do you do then? A wee conundrum.

So decide now how many of you in your family will be involved in the graduation book preparation or if anybody else will even know it exists.

Then take an empty sheet of paper and decide which of the sections in the summary (Chapter I) you want to include, plus what more you want that's not mentioned. Next, pick a rough number of photos you'd like in each section.

Add at the bottom of the page what else you need to know about (or from) the graduate so it reflects his feelings and sense of being a senior and graduating. And anything else you must gather or do to get this idea in words and on paper.

You are at the rough design time.

# SPECIAL PAGE

## The Most Important Steps

You need a whole-project checklist so the final book is ready by the target date.

Add and subtract at will, but plan, then prep, photo, and print.

- [ ] In one sentence, What's this book about?
- [ ] Who will know? Who will help?
- [ ] Lay out the contents, order, and due dates.
- [ ] Get the facts and gather available photos.
- [ ] What photos must still be taken? When? By whom?
- [ ] Lay out a sample page on your computer.
- [ ] Write the book's text.
- [ ] Select an appropriate ancillary publisher.
- [ ] Finalize the bound interior file for submission.

[ ] Have that interior file proofread; correct errors.
[ ] Design the cover or get it designed.
[ ] Proofread the cover and submit it.
[ ] Proof the final book sent by the publisher.
[ ] When it's as you want it, give it an OK.
[ ] If you want an e-book, convert the bound book text file into an acceptable digital format.
[ ] Create an e-book front cover.
[ ] Submit both to the e-book publisher.
[ ] Proof the e-book too. Give it an OK.
[ ] When the book(s) arrive(s), have a party!
[ ] Oops, it's too late to appear on Oprah with other book creators. Strut anyway.

Chapter 3

## Must you do it alone?

Of course not.

But that is your first choice to make, particularly if it's to be a surprise to the grad. Every time you add another collaborator, you double the likelihood that the beans will be spilled. By graduation time, it may be the worst kept secret in town!

The second choice was already mentioned, that you and the grad are partners in the quest. Then you must ask whether you two will keep that a secret, so the book will be a surprise to the rest of the family, or who else can know, if they ask or are interested. Or will you broadcast the grand venture early on so the rest (of the world) can get involved?

That is the third choice, that many will know. Should that include your spouse, or the grandparents, or even the other kids? How much pressure will their knowing put on you, intentionally or inadvertently? Will too many chefs sour the stew?

There are other variables too. Since you need some simple computer skills and experience to produce and lay out the book's text and photos in a planned, consistent format, you might selectively choose specific family members or friends for digital help. The same for photos, relying on them to take enough top quality photos and to store the originals and back-ups.

There is a fourth choice. You intend to go it alone, or with a co-conspirator, but as time goes on you need more help and/or you need to get the graduate aboard. Then you add personnel as needed. But no loose lips—and the most important thing is that the book be super.

A fifth choice takes a pinch more organization but might even be more fun. Why not a cluster of mothers or a pride of papas getting together a few hours a week to pool resources and wits, each to create their own kid's grad book? The group might even be, heavens forfend, a mix of both sexes. Will that inevitably lead to cross-photography, taking shots of the others' child? Or other untoward acts like pooling funds on a cover design? (Mum's the word.)

"A milestone passed,
new things begun,
drama as shining as the sun,
a goal achieved, a victory won!
That's Graduation!"

      Anonymous


"And will you succeed?
Yes! You will indeed!
(98 and ¾ percent guaranteed)"

      Dr. Seuss (1904-1981)

Chapter 4

## A checklist and a timetable are invaluable...

If this book is to be about a specific high school graduation and graduate, at least you can calculate the closing date of our book's prep time.

Let's assume there is a ceremony practice, the actual graduation a day or two later, a party somewhere that night, and maybe a gathering or two within the next couple of days. Say that it's a typical June rite and all of the above winds up on June 10. Add a few foot-dragging days and your publication date is by or before June 15.

For clarification, if the book and cover are digitally submitted that day, the e-book will surely be out in e-book form by the next day. The bound book may take 10-14 days to arrive in bound perfection.

Only you know the precise starting prep date. I should imagine you'll want to give yourself at least two or three months minimum before June 15. If so, that provides you with an exact production window. Or you could start 6-12 months before graduation, if you wish. But one date is certain: the closing date is June 15.

## The checklist

Next, you have to divide the to-do tasks into sections, and then give each element of the sections a deadline date.

It's pretty hard to go wrong if tasks are completed before their deadlines; weeks or even months early are blessings. But being late can be a disaster.

Let's create a quick checklist for a simple version of such a graduation book to see why the timing is critical.

Let's say you decide to build the book around the graduate, his family, his friends, the senior prom, the actual ceremony, and the related parties. The graduate is Ben and his girlfriend, who is also graduating, is Betty.

Here's how a bare-bones checklist might appear:

## Ben, the graduate

| item | text | X | pix | specifics |
|---|---|---|---|---|
| Ben as kid | 1-p bio | | 3-5 | baby, about 8, at 12 |
| schools | 1 p | | 4 | 1 pix @ school |
| where lived | 1 p | | 3 | 1 pix @ home + 1 his room |
| bike + car | | | 2 | 1 pix of each |
| sports | 2 pp | | 4 | cross country, BB, track |
| Ben in gown | 2-pp bio | | 1-2 | high school days |

## Ben's family

| item | text | X | pix | specifics |
|---|---|---|---|---|
| | 2 pp | | 1 | family history, full family photo at graduation |
| father | total, | | 1 | pix of @ at graduation time |
| mother | 2 pp | | 1 | |
| brother | bio | | 1 | |
| sister | | | 1 | |
| Buster, dog | ½ p bio | | 3 | 1 of dog and Ben, 2 of dog |
| Papa Jones | ½ p bio | | 1 | grandfather |
| Smiths | ½ p bio | | 1 | grandparents |
| GG Lily | ½ p bio | | 1 | great-grandmother |
| | 1 p bio | | 3 | uncles, aunts, cousins |

## Senior prom, Ben and Betty

| item | text | X | pix | specifics |
|---|---|---|---|---|
| prom photo | 2-3 pp | | 1 | |
| dancing | | | 1 | |
| at table | | | 1 | |
| swimming | | | 1 | |

## Ben's graduation ceremony

| item | text | X | pix | specifics |
|---|---|---|---|---|
| calendar | 1 full p | | | .gif of schedule |
| cap-gown | 3 pp text | | 1 | trying them on |
| pre-ceremony | | | 1 | |
| overview | | | 1 | view of auditorium set up |
| Ben getting diploma | | | 1 | as he is handed his diploma |
| Ben and Betty | | | 1 | both in gowns/caps |
| Ben with family | | | 1 | after ceremony |

| | | | | | |
|---|---|---|---|---|---|
| Ben + @ g/parent | | | 3 | with gown/cap | |
| Ben + friends | | | 2 | with school friends | |

**Ben's graduation parties:**

| item | text | X | pix | specifics |
|---|---|---|---|---|
| that night | ½ p text | | 3 | with friends |
| next day, at home | 3 pp text | | 2 | with extended family |
| " " | | | 1 | list/pix of guests |
| " " | | | 1 | list/pix of family attending |
| next night, at Betty's | ½ p text | | 2 | Betty's family + both grads |

You have five sections of the book, each with inexact amounts of copy (interior text) and photos, with some breakdown of what you'd like to see in the book (in the "item" and "specifics" columns).

A quick tally gives you about 25 pages of text, 58 photos (pix) max, and about 6-7 more pages in the front and between sections. If each photo takes a full page (it won't since some will be embedded in the text), you would have a book 90-100 pages long.

If there are 200 words a page that means somebody must write about 5,000 words of stirring, grammatically correct prose about 18 different topics. Which in turn means that there must be some fact-finding involved.

And someone must take (or find) 58 photos, 21 of which are historical, one is a .gif (of the graduation schedule), and most of the rest can be taken live at the ceremony or parties.

The most difficult part will be finding the older photos and getting them scanned up to acceptable print level.

Still, while the writing and photo posting will be a new adventure, this book requires nothing that is overwhelming or even especially challenging. The biggest task is just doing it and getting those X boxes checked off in a predictable fashion.

The photos have three potential fates: (1) they are must-do assignments, (2) if not taken, that segment will be deleted, or (3) the visual will not appear but the related text might. The most critical photos are from the prom, the graduation, and from the parties afterward. So those tasks must be assigned to the most reliable helper. Extra photos must be taken in each case too (to select the best), and they must be gathered into the final book quickly before deadline day.

Another caveat: if there is a professional photographer taking shots, you can't count on using or including that photography. In fact, without getting permission and probably paying a goodly sum, you can't use it at all. Thus the prom and graduation photos must be taken by you or a designee.

## The timetable

What's missing in the checklist is the "when."

You can create one more column, perhaps following the "specifics," that includes the date by which that item must (or at least should) be completed.

Let's say you have a three-month window from start to finish, say (A) March 15-April 15, (B) April 15-May 15, and (C) May 15-June 15, and you assign letters to each (for your sake here).

In the (A) period, you could complete all of the text writing and pix gathering about Ben except the photo of him in his gown. You might also finish "Ben's family" too, though you might have to wait until the ceremony, if they are attending, to get current photos of the older (and newest) family members.

Assuming that the senior prom is in the (B) period, that's when you could complete that section, as well as get a copy and reproduce the graduation calendar, when it's available. (If the school doesn't have an usable calendar, create your own on your computer, then save it in PDF.)

Then (C) will be dedicated, no-nonsense, to getting the copy quickly written about the graduation and the postgrad parties, with lots of sharp photos to bring that back alive 20 or 30 years later!

Another very important action must be applied to all of the text after it is written and before it is submitted to the publisher: it must be proofread by an experienced outsider. Why? Because each error will be preserved for decades and will increase the target's threshold of embarrassment, with your name also on it—as the author who didn't know better! There's a cure. Just let fresh, trained eyes give a last okay. (Alas, another person in the growing corps of secret-keepers!)

## What if changes are necessary?

Great, if they improve the graduation book, make it better, easier to read, clearer to view...

Just remember what every long-time writer or publisher learns: only you knew what you originally had in mind. So if a picture of Ben's second dog just can't be found or if you can only use two party photos because the others are too fuzzy to distinguish humans, no problem. Don't complain or mention it. The book is a few photos shorter.

The same with the copy. What goes in must work. Leave out what doesn't.

For example, this book isn't the place to stir bad feelings, belabor painful shortcomings, or do anything but feature positive accomplishments and herald a grand event.

If Ben graduated dead last and was just rejected by all of the branches of the military, that is your secret (and

Ben's). It isn't mentioned. What is read in this book must be as welcome and embracing at the tenth and fiftieth anniversary of the graduation as it was on that special day.

It's about time to hang some words on the skeleton.

SPECIAL PAGE

## Sample Book Text

This is how your book text might read:

**Great Grandma Lily**

"GG" is 89 (less a day) as Ben graduates. She graduated from Taft High School in Akron, Ohio, in 1941, just as Hitler invaded the Soviet Union in World War II. Lilith Annett Carter married Ben's great grandfather Leo six months later, a few weeks before he enlisted in the Navy and went almost immediately to the Pacific Theater. They had five kids: Mom (Rita), Alice, Linda, Leo Jr., and Pancredo Leon (Uncle Pan). "GG" plays a wicked game of cards.

## Betty and Frank Smith

Photo of the Smiths

Ben's grandparents on his Dad's side live two blocks away as Ben gets his diploma. They also went to Central City High and graduated on the same stage as Ben, in 1959. Betty was a high school cheerleader before becoming the journalism teacher at CCH. Frank lettered three years in baseball at CCH. He worked in seven different city jobs before retiring last year as the Director of Parks and Recreation.

Chapter 5

# Finding the words to create a fun masterpiece

This book may be about Ben but it has two other stars that must perform or poor Ben will perish from blushing. Those other stars are the words and the photos.

Of the two, the words get top billing. You can get by with six or eight sort-of-clear photos, just so one shows a happy (and identifiable) Ben in graduation garb.

But you can't just shuffle through the text, taking pot shots at the spelling and running rampant with the grammar.

Still, you needn't be much concerned in the beginning. The big stuff is getting the text on paper and in the right location. A fussy old aunt or a high school English teacher can proofread the final body into perfection.

## Do it like the professionals

Odd as it sounds, professional writers (who make a good living from wordsmithing) learn real early that the most important thing is to get the words down while the spirit is on them.

Article writers, for example, create a simple outline and do the research, then just write the sections like they are talking to an interested (but fairly uninformed) friend. In other words, they just get the facts and related text down on paper so it makes sense.

That means no editing, no rewriting, just putting all of the words down in a rough first draft.

When that's done, they reread that draft (still no editing) and they (1) move things around if they make more sense in a different order and (2) they fill in any of the gaps they overlooked, aren't clear, or need more text to be fully understood.

When that first draft is as good as it can get, they go through it word by word and edit it up to perfection. They check the spelling (particularly names), the punctuation, the agreement of verbs and nouns, and pronoun clarity. At the same time they lean it out, pruning unneeded, redundant, or imprecise words or phrases, so it reads fast and makes immediate sense.

Finally, the proofreader is given this ready-to-go final second draft, upon which she works her magic. The end result is the book you will gift your child, a book so spotless not a relative alive can fault you for not having passed English with an A+. (Even if they sat next to you in class and know the real truth.)

**Mostly, just do it.**

What that means here is that you print out a copy of your Checklist and your Timetable and you just get going, putting the ideas and words down on paper or in your computer so you can check off each timetable item.

Who cares what order you attack and complete them? Want to write about Ben and sports first, and you need a couple of immodest pages to do that justice? Go to it. Maybe a hundred-word bio (a half page) of Great-grandma Lily next? Have at it! Ready to write about Buster the dog? Bark away!

You'll just rearrange the copy in the right order later. Get the words down now. Confirm the facts, check the dates (if needed), and put the words on paper or screen.

If you are starting out, say, with Ben's youth, you might dig out the photos and use them as memory-prods to prep a one-page bio of young Ben. How many words a page? Say 200-250. (Use your "word count[er]" in the Tools section.)

What if you can't think of more than 100 words—or even 20? Poor Ben! But don't panic, it will just be a shorter page and book.

But what if you can't do it in less than 550 words? Write and leave it for now. You can adjust the actual words and pages later. 550 words are fine. It's writing time now. You will edit and prune later. Far better to have too many words than none.

## What if you don't know what Ben thinks?

Both approaches to writing—objective or subjective—can work in this book.

Since the objective approach doesn't include Ben's feelings, what he thinks is irrelevant. That's very important if he doesn't know you are preparing the book as a graduation gift. Otherwise you'd either have to guess how he feels or you'd have to pull it out of him with parental guile—that he'd probably see right through!

For example, let's say you are writing about the three houses Ben lived in as a kid.

In objective writing you would tell the reader about the three houses, where they were, what was Ben's age when he lived there, and maybe a special thing he had or enjoyed while he was there, like the horse pasture at the first house, the boat dock at the second, and having his own room in the attic where he lives now.

Subjective writing can be more difficult because Ben's feelings expressed in the book might change later (but the book won't). And not everything is subjective. (You will describe the family members objectively.) Still, if you use that format, you would ask Ben what he thought about the houses where he grew up, with some facts included so the reader knows what he is talking about.

That's the problem. If Ben is a typical teenage boy, when you ask him how he feels about the houses where he grew up, his most likely response will be "Uh, I don't know. Never thought about it. I guess they were great." Not much of a chapter!

## What's the best way to write the text?

Let's answer that in reverse. What does the final text (or book copy) look like when it's sent to the publisher?

It looks like the insides of a book, typed on a computer and set up just like the pages you finally want to read.

First, figure out the size you want your graduation book to be. It would be great to have it 8 ½" x 11", the size of a legal pad, wouldn't it? Lots of room for photos and copy. But you probably can't afford that for the simple reason that almost none of the ancillary publishers print books that large. Why? It's the amount of paper involved (you pay for paper) and the weight of the book, plus the reality that libraries and bookstores have trouble displaying them on their shelves.

A much more affordable size and one that all of the publishers offer is a book measured 6" x 9." That means that if you set your page in your software to that size, and you move the copy in by one inch on all four sides so your actual typing space will be 4" x 7".

Now you need a type font. Use a serif face; good choices might be Verdana, Times New Roman, or Century—the same font throughout. And a size that is readable but not too big. Why not 11 point? You can add a footer (page number and book title) in a bound book by going to View/Header and Footer and typing the information in the footer box. (Also open the Page Setup box there, go to Layout, then check Different first page.) Decide if you will indent paragraphs, if the text will be lined up (justified) at the beginning and end of each sentence, and the size of the section headings (maybe 13 or 14 point bold face).

You need an example? Look at the very page you are reading now: 6" x 9", same layout dimensions, Verdana 11 point for the body text (Verdana 14 Bold for the chapter heads), paragraphs indented (except the first in each chapter), justified right and left, with a footer.

Set up the page size (in File/Page Setup). Then start typing. What you see before you is more or less how the bound book will appear. Remember to save your work regularly. Isn't this book writing easy?

**Must you create an e-book too?**

Probably not for a high school graduation book, but you can do it fairly easily (see the guidelines below).

The best thing about a digital book is that it's easy to make once you have the copy finished for the bound book. The links are live, the photos will be in full color, and they can be zoomed up to much larger sizes.

And it's free. All the relatives or friends have to do is add the link you provide to their computer (or handheld device) and they can see the entire book instantly.

Of course, you have to save the copy and photos on that link, and you may want it stored on some website, but free portals can be found by asking Google.com and moving the file to a new home. Or you can just add the link as an attachment to an e-mail sent to all those who are delighted (perhaps amazed) with Ben's graduation.

**How does the digital copy differ?**

It's mostly the same digital file of the bound book we are talking about now.

But you must make some modifications so the ancillary publishers (like Smashwords and Kindle) can package and send it. That is, the original text must be modified to fit into their software pagination and image-reproducing limitations. Mostly that requires removing footers, headers, and page numbers throughout, including the table of contents and the index. It also requires you to check the files for pagebreak glitches. And because the reader can directly link to references in e-books, you will likely change www... addresses into direct links, which the reader can activate. Also, it's best to reduce your font to nothing larger than 12 point throughout the e-book.

Make a copy of your bound book file, add "dig" (no quote signs) to the file title (like mydigbook.doc) and make the necessary changes. Then save this modified "dig" file as a PDF file and retitle it again, keeping the "dig" in the title and ending it with .pdf. This file will then become the master file for many of the digital versions to be sold through all of the ancillary publishing companies.

**You have two books ready to go!**

You will end up with two large files, each containing all of the contents of the interior parts of the book, one for the bound book, the other for the digital. Add to that the respective book covers, and in those four files you will have the entire book in both formats. That is what you will submit to the publisher(s) you select. They will walk you through the submissions—as will I for both Lulu and CreateSpace in Chapter 11.

## Some final writing thoughts.

Keep the prose tight; don't repeat the same word in the same sentence (or paragraph) unless it's "Ben," a conjunction, or a preposition; limit paragraphs to two or three sentences; avoid run-on sentences, and stick to the theme of that section.

Ben, your family, and the world are eager to know about the graduation and about things directly related, like Ben's childhood, his friends, and the graduation ceremony and festivities.

But that's it. Don't make Ben any more a hero than he really is, though he must be every bit as special and important as the moment requires.

Keep the writing upbeat, fact-filled, and properly concise. It's about Ben, and a bit about Betty, Ben's family, and his first 18 or so years.

Just get the words down and keep the sentences short. Double-check all the facts. Get it proofed.

Mostly, though, it's about doing the writing. That's the place at which most well-intentioned books disappear.

But not here!

Congratulations, you are about to become a published author!

Chapter 6

# Do you need anybody's permission?

New writers are afraid that any person they quote or photo will turn around and sue them for, who knows, millions of dollars—and probably tack on 10 or 20 years in jail.

Book writers or publishers are the worst of the lot, until they catch on. (Then they still don't believe it.)

Talking about the written text first, what you write (the words and quotes) is almost suit-proof if you just tell the truth and use the words as said (or close). Thus, interviews recorded (digital recorders are the least obtrusive way) provide the strongest evidence, if ever needed, that what you are sharing in print is a faithful rendition of what was said.

You can also take good notes by hand at the time of the interview, or even pull it all together reasonably soon afterward. Again, if the book's contents clearly convey the facts and message intended, that's all you need.

(How do I know? Most of the 1,700+ freelance articles I've had in print included one or several interviewees, with a majority coming from pre-recorder days. Hand notes that I almost always typed out the same day while I could remember the exchange. There was never a wisp of a legal challenge.)

You probably won't conduct many interviews for a high school graduation book. Most of the facts and observations will come from first-hand inspection or from written reports or accounts. If you preserve the accuracy of those sources, you need no further permission.

Anyway, many of the people interviewed will be Ben's family, friends, teachers, or from Betty. Rather than sue you, they will be so happy to be part of a real book they'd probably pay you just to be included, rather than the reverse because they are there!

Incidentally, you don't need their permission to ask them questions or to use the answers—again, assuming you use their words truthfully. But it makes a lot of sense to tell them what's going on at the outset—"a short history of Ben's high school days" if you don't want to spill the grad book beans—when you take out the recorder or your notepad. Not telling them what you are doing is far more likely to fan their suspicion and tighten their lips.

Photos can be a bit testier. Including pictures of little kids or full-blown adult paranoids would make me the most nervous. I'd probably have them sign a photo release (the parents for the kids), if possible. That would probably give me more ease of mind.

But, again, I must have had 2,000+ photos accompanying those 1,700+ articles sold (most about travel), and I recall only getting about ten photo releases—and no complaints (or law suits) ever. And I was easy to find too: just contact the publication.

So let's put Ben's high school graduation book in perspective. The photos you'll take will be of his (and your) family, his buddies, the school, some public shots of the graduation itself, and maybe some historical photos of his old houses and pets.

In fact, most of the star characters will be minors (most won't be 18 or older) so in fact that does raise the issue of "kids" in the jpgs!

So you have two choices, really. Assume that the other graduates or students would be delighted to appear in every shot, then maybe have a copy of each photo with that person it to give them, in thanks, after you gift the book to Ben.

Or you can run off a batch of photo releases to give to the minors (and their folks for signature) who appear in the book, just for ease of mind.

I wouldn't worry about the older adults and your family.

Remember that you don't need permission if the photos are taken in or from a public place. If lots of others are taking photos, particularly at the school and the ceremonies, you can do it too.

At the end of this chapter is a link to a photo release form you might want to use. You can simply inject your name rather than the National Park Service, rewrite the model, and use it forever.

What I am sharing about photos and releases here is from years of on-site experience, and it's what I do. But—yes, the disclaimer—I'm not a lawyer so if you have any legal questions, talk to an actual lawyer to settle your mind. (It doesn't count that I once posed as a lawyer in a friend's slide show.)

Mostly, just get this very limited circulation book together and distribute it to the people you love.

---

**Model photo release form:** http://nbii-nin.ciesin.columbia.edu/jamaicabay/bioblitz/NPS_PhotoReleaseForm.pdf

**SPECIAL PAGE**

# How the Printed Text Looks

This book, as you see it, was written and set as a Word file, so it suffers from having too much space between the words where hyphenation won't help. For example, if you use the word "thought" near the end of a sentence, you'll have holes. See what I mean?

If that loose spacing doesn't bother you, it's a lot cheaper just to do it yourself and suffer a bit. (Just don't tell the others; they may never notice.)

But if you want your book to look more professional, you can find a book designer and see how they can improve your final book (and probably do a better job with photo placement). They may have solid suggestions before you prepare your final pages too. Just get a bid so you know the additional costs in advance.

Using a smaller type font also helps tighten the spacing. (11 point)

Using a smaller type font also helps tighten the spacing. See. (9 point)

Chapter 7

## A collective venture?

I've mentioned this before, but producing a high school graduation book might be even more fun if it's done with neighbors or other parents with kids about to get their educational walking papers!

The two biggest problems are both related to the secrecy of the gift tome(s).

First, it's hard to get the word out to other parents without those pesky kids finding out. High schoolers are great at snagging notes. And you can hardly announce your true intentions in the local or school newspaper.

Second, it's probably harder to secretly gather on the odd night to work together or compare progress. Again, kids are experts at intrigue or sneaking off, so if you try it, good luck!

Having said the obvious, if you want to gather a friend or several, all with the intent of creating their own books, then you might use this book's rough outline to mark your progress points.

Nothing is more important than the plan for each book, mostly how big you each want your books to be and what deadlines you must meet to have them printed a few days after the ceremony.

Once outlines are drawn up for the books, most of what's left is digging up the facts, getting or taking photos, and inserting the components into the interior (contents) file, which is the books' digital skeleton and running repository.

Folks usually need the most help getting their computer to do what they want. Page design, fonts, type size, hyphenation, photo cropping and insertion, and the rest. So if one of the group is more knowledgeable or experienced there, their sharing of the how-to ways is a godsend.

In fact, the group might divide up the tasks according to their expertise or interests. That is, one person might keep, say, all three books digitally stored on their computer, showing the others how text can be sent or exchanged as needed.

Another might be the photographer in charge of taking informal portrait shots, some in the gown, and of course the main photos at the ceremony. (Each person would be responsible for finding their respective historical family photos, if needed. And maybe some pre- and post-party photos too.)

Their meeting together might help prod each person to complete task deadlines on time, as well as providing an advice and sounding board. If outside guidance would be beneficial, of course it's much easier to bring an expert to meet all of the book developers at once than one at a time.

Let me introduce heresy. If there are three book creators in the group, they might even consider developing just one book with three stars—their own graduates!

## SPECIAL PAGE

## Copyright

*Ben Barker's High School Graduation Book* is one of a kind, unless there's another Ben Barker afoot matching suit! Anyway, nobody can "copyright" titles.

What you need to do is get a copy of Ben's opus into the Library of Congress and protected, as is, for all time.

How is that done? By registering the copyright. To do that you need a TX form, which you can download directly from the following link, then mail:

http://www.gov/forms/formtx.pdf

Fill out the TX, pay $35, and mail two copies of the best form (if it's in both bound and digital forms, send the bound copies) to the address indicated. You can't complete the process before the book is printed.

That's it. That makes the book official and strengthens its legal copyright protection.

Chapter 8

## Picking the best free publisher

Let's talk about publishers for a minute. The big New York houses aren't interested in Ben's graduation, and frankly nor are their many smaller cousins in every corner of America. The reason is obvious: in their business model there's no money to be made from selling 20 or 30 copies.

Your next choice might be to set up your own publishing house, put the book together, and have 25 copies run by a P.O.D. printer—or 1,000 copies by offset printing. But to do that you must learn about publishing, fulfillment, and the rest of it. (I started in 1982 learning that and I'm still learning!)

But the reason I'm writing this book is because a small miracle occurred for folks like us. A few years back a half dozen companies appeared that would professionally publish your book, text and cover, free (or nearly), creating the digit copy almost immediately, and the bound version in a week or 10 days. They would also sell the book, make it accessible to any person or store in a couple of days (in print), and would give you a royalty of 30-85% of those sales.

Even better, they would print almost any kind of decent book that was laid out in book form and had a cover, if it was submitted to them so it fit into their production system. That includes high school graduation books like Ben's!

At first I didn't believe it. Their new structure and promises were so different there had to be a trick. So I tried it (I now have 14 books out through them) and it's legitimate, though the royalty returns are very modest. (It's ideal for Ben's book because the cash back isn't the reason for the publication.)

## What are the ancillary publishers?

Here are the companies offering this service as this book is written:

    CreateSpace, createspace.com
        (bound books)

Lulu, lulu.com (bound and e-books)
Blurb, blurb.com (bound books, mostly art)
PubIt!, pubit.com (bound books)
Kindle, https://kdp.amazon.com (e-books)
Smashwords, smashwords.com (e-books, including iPad and Sony)
Scribd, scribd.com (e-books, mostly reports)

Lightning Source, lightningsource.com (bound and e-books)

You are invited to go to any of the websites listed above to see how their services work. You will need the name of your book to get in, but then you can enter approximate numbers to navigate through and test the process, leaving at any point along the way.

Why is LightningSource isolated a bit on the bottom? Because while it does sell bound and e-books (its mother company is Ingram, a huge distributor), it is more a place to get small P.O.D. (print-on-demand) printing runs. And its services aren't free, as they are in the seven firms listed before it. The setup fee is $75 for the text and cover, plus $30 to ship the proof. So it's not the place to begin, but worth strong consideration later if your book sells well and you want to lay in your own stock.

For Ben's graduation tome, since commercial sales are at best secondary, I would suggest starting at CreateSpace (an Amazon firm that is the easiest of the list to use) or at Lulu, where both a bound and digital book are created from the same files. Both provide a free ISBN number, which you probably don't want since your book's not being sold commercially—but since they are expensive, that's a sizable savings.

The process couldn't be simpler. Check each website and see what they provide and what you must do to participate as you are writing your book. Decide which publisher you want to use. Get the interior and cover files finished and proofed. Submit the files and related information; read the onscreen proof carefully. If the book looks as you want it, tell them to mail you the printed proof. Approve it, or correct it and proof the book again. That will cost from about $10 to $25 for the mailing.

You're done!

Along the way each site will tell you how much the final books will cost, and how much you might think of charging (you set the price).

Why did I suggest CreateSpace and Lulu? The last three of the seven houses don't print bound books, Blurb does (and the craftsmanship is excellent) but they are very expensive and they produce mostly art books. PubIt! is new (from Barnes and Noble) and I have too little experience with its publishing branch to recommend it. But by all means check them out!

My only reservation sending you off to the publishers untethered? None of the seven have a straightforward process that even a semi-techie can go through without confusion. I went through the submission maze at all of the houses several times before I deciphered their directions and found the unprovided answers.

In fact, I wrote *How to Get Your Book Published Free in Minutes and Marketed Worldwide in Days* specifically to explain this whole process, then to take the daring by the hand and walk them through all of the submission paths (except PubIt!) so they could get their works listed and selling without throwing their hands in the air and fleeing. So if that would help you, please get the book (almost all of the ancillary publishers sell it, as do we). See the details at

www.mybookpublishedinminutes.com

Chapter 9

# Inserting the photos to match the text

The second most important part of the high school graduation book is the photos.

In fact, many folks have at best one or two photos of their graduation. Most just have their yearbook grad photo—if their school had yearbooks, if they posed for it, and if they can find the tome! (As a last resort, there is likely a copy in the library in the town where your high school was located.)

So what makes your graduation book truly unique is the combination of the photos and the prose: a real once-in-a-lifetime see-and-tell masterpiece.

## Do you need a special camera?

Just the same good digital camera that you use for all events should work. You can still use a 35mm film camera too—if you can find film and get it developed.

But the cameras in your hand phone or iPad are probably too small and inexact for this project.

Digital cameras are far easier to use, in part because you can review each shot on the camera after it is taken. If what you see isn't what you want, you can continue taking more photos until one or several are acceptable.

When you have the shot(s) you need, you can usually directly link the camera to your computer (with a USB or a cord/insert attachment) to transfer (download) the .jpg files. Each file contains a color photo you took. Those files can also easily be converted into black-and-white.

### Should you take vertical or horizontal shots?

When you design the grad book's contents you will need sufficient space to include the text and artwork (mostly photos).

You will probably create a "dummy" layout book on paper, with a model design for each page. The first draft needn't be full size. A sample page of the family biographies and pix might look like this:

| Ben's parents... | |
|---|---|
| photo of Ben's mother | photo of Ben's father |
| **Marge Jones** | **Harold Jones** |
| xxxxxxxxxxxx xxxxxxxxxxxx xxxxxxxxxxxx xxxxxxxxxxxx xxxxxxxxxxxx xxxxxxxxxxxx xxxxxxxxxxxx xxxxxxxxxxxx | xxxxxxxxxx xxxxxxxxxx xxxxxxxxxx xxxxxxxxxx xxxxxxxxxx xxxxxxxxxx xxxxxxxxxx xxxxxxxxxx |

The xxx sections are where the text copy will appear, and the "photo of" boxes are where the respective .jpg pix will be inserted in the submission file (use Insert, Picture, From file).

In this example, plan to use a horizontal photo for each, although a vertical photo may work as well if the height of the box is expanded.

But remember that you are paper planning here, and if you end up with two fairly tall photos you could easily redesign the page to look like this:

**Ben's parents...**

photo of
Ben's mother

**Marge Jones**

xxxxxxxxxxxx
xxxxxxxxxxxx
xxxxxxxxxxxx
xxxxxxxxxxxx
xxxxxxxxxxxx
xxxxxxxxxxxx
xxxxxxxxxxxx
xxxxxxxxxxx

| | **Harold Jones** |
|---|---|
| photo of Ben's father | xxxxxxxxxxxx xxxxxxxxxxxx xxxxxxxxxxxx xxxxxxxxxxxx xxxxxxxxxxxx xxxxxxxxxxxx xxxxxxxxxxxx |

The point is, you have flexibility regarding where the photos appear and how the copy is laid out around or near them. It's your book and you get to use the space as you wish. The real restrictors are the size of the type you will use (for comfortable reading) and the minimum size the photos must be so Ben, his buddies, and his parents can be clearly seen.

Thus the easiest way to handle the photos so you have the greatest flexibility is to take at least several clear shots in both horizontal and vertical form. Rest assured that a top professional publisher would insist on several *dozen* photos for each layout—and *Na-*

*tional Geographic* might require several *hundred* for each photo used! The moral: too many pix both tall and fat may still be too few!

**Some photo guidelines**

\* Clarity is the golden rule. You only have one chance to capture Ben, Betty, friends, and family on these pages, so every time they appear everybody in the photo should be clearly identifiable and it must be obvious what they are doing.

\* If the setting is also important (like the front of the school or Ben crossing the graduation stage to receive a (false) diploma, that too must be clear.

\* Full-lens photos usually work best, with you moving closer or farther away to include what's desired in the shot.

\* Wide-angle or tight, zoomed shots sometimes work well but always check the shots in the camera to see if the lighting and details are acceptable.

\* Remember that you can crop photos to fit them into your paste box (where they will appear in your book). That means you can move one, two, or even all four borders of the final shot closer together to reduce the area finally used in the book.

* You can also lighten or darken your shots, although it's much better to get the needed light and contrast in the original photo. You use Photo Shop or similar editing software to create the best setting. Make changes at some peril since each time you do so the photo becomes progressively (and permanently) grainier.

## How do you actually find and fit in the photos?

Let's say you take 100 digital photos and you save them in your computer in My Pictures files in a folder called "Ben's Graduation Book."

Each photo will have a file name, like P1000105.JPG. Let's imagine that one is the shot of Ben, cape and cap, shaking hands with his Dad, and it's one you want to use. It's a vertical shot but you want it half that size.

So you find the file on your computer and click it so that Ben in all his glory appears on the screen. Is it usable?

You must "shrink" that photo by 50%.

There are four ways to do that. One, you highlight the photo that you have on your work page. You will see small black boxes along the margins of the photo. Go to any corner and move the box toward the center. The photo will shrink in all directions until you stop. So here you can move the box until the photo is half as wide—the size you want. But is it tall enough or is it too tall?

The second way, if it is too tall, is to prune the photo just mentioned by moving the top or bottom border down or up, thus shortening the photo to the size you want. But doing so might distort the photo that's left. And you might decapitate Ben, cut him off at the knees, or make him fat or short.

The third way is to go to the photo editing tools and actually crop the shot, eliminating parts of the photo from either side, the top, the bottom, or any combination, until you have a shot size that works ).

For example, here is a photo of a garish plastic parrot that I reduced by cropping:

How did I do that? I created a copy of the shot on the left by putting the mouse over the photo and right clicking. In the box that appeared, I hit the word "copy." Then I opened a blank page and put the cursor on that blank page, pushed the right side of my mouse, and hit the "paste" key. Voilá, the parrot flew to my new page!

But I didn't need the branches at the top nor the white blossoms to the right—just the parrot. So I right clicked my mouse, with the cursor on the pasted photo, and a box opened and one of the choices was "Show Picture Toolbar." In that toolbar I found the "crop" tool, and on the eight black dots that appeared in the frame of the new pasted picture, I pushed the left mouse, put the tool over the dot on the top in the middle and moved down until I had the height I wanted. Then I did the same on the middle dot on the right of the photo, moving the crop tool left until I had the width I needed. So the photo on the left, above, became the reduced photo on the right, without any distortion. (I copied the smaller photo on the empty page and pasted it in the right table cell, as you see above.) I also saved that smaller photo on an "empty" page so I could use it later.

The fourth way is to have several or many different sizes of the photo you need so that among the clear choices there is one that can be sized to fit your book!

## How many photos do you need?

Maybe only one: Ben in his gown and cap smiling and pointing at his diploma!

Maybe two: the one mentioned plus a full-class shot of the entire group of graduates.

Maybe three: those plus Ben actually being handed his diploma on the stage.

Who knows? It's your book, you pick. If you pick 38 and you have 38 sharp photos that show what you want, then 38 is the perfect number.

But if you end up with 28 photos that deserve to be shared in print, then you may wisely modify the layout, share what you can, and either expand the copy or adjust and shorten the book.

The fireworks begin today.
Each diploma is a lighted match.
Each one of you is a fuse."

Edward Koch (1924-   )
former Mayor of New York City


"There is a good reason why they
call these ceremonies
'commencement exercises.'
Graduation is not the end,
it's the beginning."

Senator Orrin Hatch (1934-   )

Chapter 10

## Creating a fast, free cover

Every book deserves a cover!

But we're going to give your book two or three—one on the front, another on the back, and the third (if the book is thick enough) on the spine.

Your back cover will probably be blank (though you can decorate it however you wish). And the spine will only have type on it (the book's title and perhaps the author's name) if the book includes, usually, 100 (better 130) or more pages.

So let's focus on the front cover here.

You have two software choices regarding its design and composition: (1) you can use the publisher's software or (2) you can use other software and save the design and text in PDF format, to submit to the publisher when they request the cover.

Whether you design it yourself, you hire a cover designer, you do it by committee, or you prefer something even more fanciful, at some point some cover must be provided before the book will be printed.

After you submit the cover file to your chosen publisher, you will see a copy of that cover at that time. You will see it again as you approve the book for the proof printing, and again when the proof arrives by mail for your final OK.

You can modify the cover (file) at each of those steps. And you can change it again any time after the book has been proofed and printed, though that stops the printing process until you go through the submission process another time.

As you can imagine, the earlier in the process that you make changes, the better. In fact, because a graduation book is time-sensitive (it gets progressively less critical the longer your book appears after the graduation), it makes particular sense to do it once and right the first time!

**This cover is really easy to do!**

Fortunately, this is an easy cover to compose.

Mostly, it needs a purpose, a name, a date, maybe a place, perhaps a photo, and possibly some design do-dads.

Let's invent that data:

> Purpose: High School Graduation Book
> Name: Ben Barker
> Date: June 5, 2030
> Place: Central City High School
> Photo: either Ben in grad garb or some shot of the ceremony with Ben centrally located
> Do-dads: maybe some border lace or a mortar board with tassel top center in the background

Oh yes, it needs some contrasting colors to at least make the copy visible and legible.

So let's put these pieces together and create a starter cover. Since I have almost no artistic sense, readers are invited to beg for instant improvement.

Still, you must start somewhere. How about this?

# Ben Barker

**High School Graduation 2030**

Central City High School
Central City, Iowa

The (red) horizontal boxes at the top and bottom are do-dads. I've not included the author's name on the cover, though it will properly appear on the first page, with the inside title.

You don't see any colors inside the bound version of this heart-stopper but in the book's cover that you are preparing you can have any colors you want. (You could even see the inside colors in the e-book.)

For example, the boxes and the name Ben Barker might be scarlet red, the background white, and the photo in full color—as they are in reality.

The cover's background might be one solid tone that complements the other colors used. Or it could be black with stars twinkling throughout (with the black text reversed in white), or the background a rainbow moving from bright to light as it changes hues. (The back and spine often have the same background colors too.)

Or the background may be as white as this page.

## Who will be involved in the cover design?

Will you clandestinely create the entire book all by yourself? Wow! Great.

Or will you quietly find a computer-savvy, design-sensitive soul to put the cover together (and maybe the inside layout too) while you write copy and take photos?

Or if the family (minus the grad) are all conspirators, you may want to have a contest among those in the know for the best cover design... You are the captain of this ship. Getting the others involved in some way creates a lifelong buy-in.

Whatever you do, more than anything the cover must be completed by deadline, which means that if others are involved (particularly artfolk), set the deadline many weeks earlier than the drop-dead date by which the book will not exist if not submitted!

## If somebody else designs your cover...

You really have three deadlines if you involve another person in the cover design.

The first is the date by which you find that designer. That should be several months before you need the final work approved and in hand.

Where might you find a designer? The phone book or on the Web. Ask friends for recommendations, particularly book publishers or adfolk. You can even check two websites where they hide: elance.com or guru.com.

The second date is when you discuss your ideas with that designer. That should be early on, maybe the very same date that you find the designer. In other words, you start looking once you have an idea of what the cover must include, what you don't want, the format the final work must come in, and whether you want to include help with the interior book layout in the same job/price.

The third can be a tier of dates: one, to see ideas or designs; the second, to see the final artwork, and the third to have the cover file in hand for insertion in the book's software. That last tier should be many weeks before the book submission must be made to the publisher.

You will also work out a fee and due dates when you design the project, and how payment is to be made. Early on, a work-for-hire agreement should be signed. This is a simple form, a page or two long, that keeps the artwork and rights in your possession.

You can usually find fill-in copies of work-for-hire agreements for purchase at your stationary store. Also, there is a free version at the following link: http://www.creativebusiness.com/pdf_free/CBworkforhire.pdf (or by checking www.google.com).

**If you use the publisher's cover software...**

Let's say you are going to produce two versions of your graduation book, a bound version and an electronic (e-book) version. And let's say that both books will be 6" x 9" in size. And that you are using an ancillary publisher so you can get the book quickly and pay almost nothing to get it published.

Mind you, you needn't create the book in both formats, but that gives me a chance here to discuss the cover both ways, then you can decide.

For an **e-book**, it couldn't be easier. You only need a front cover to send digitally as the opening page of your book. Even then, it will most likely be seen in the online catalog in thumbnail size (sizes differ for thumbnails but Google's Picasa has typical examples at 2" on the long side by 1 3/8" on the short side).

It's usually called the cover image when you save the cover for an e-book, and it can often be prepared in Word or on a Mac, then converted to PDF. (See Google to find free PDF versions if it's not already in your computer software.) Since the cover is so small in the thumbnail, the most important thing is that the title be clear and easy to read, the author's name be the same (if you include it), and any images or decorations in color stand out to be seen.

Keep it simple and well balanced. You don't include an ISBN number, a bar code, a price, or anything else on this cover image, just the title, subtitle (if any), author (if any), and the artwork.

None of the e-book ancillary publishers (Lulu, LightningSource, Kindle, Smashwords, or Scribd) provide software on their sites to help you create this cover image for the digital version. They simply want the cover in a file that you will download with the interior text of the book before you get to proof it. (You can also include the cover as the first page of your e-book so it is all entered in one file.)

So your choice is to either have it designed by someone else or to you do it yourself. You saw the simple cover produced earlier in this book. You could use that front cover again, here, for your digital book. Poor Ben will be about the size of an ant in that e-book catalog!

For a **bound book**, you only have two fill-in-the-dots ready-to-use software programs available from the ancillary publishers: at both Lulu and at

CreateSpace. For the others (Pubit!, LightningSource, and Blurb), you must design your own cover or have it designed, and when they ask you to submit the cover, you send that file. If you have it designed and you will use an ancillary publisher, have the designer go to the publisher's website and read its cover directions and dimensions.

CreateSpace is the easier of the two to use. But your cover done by either program will look like an amateur's approach to creating a cover (and both firms will imprint their name somewhere in the book or bar code).

Go to www.createspace.com, find "Create a Cover," and hit the first question mark in the upper right hand corner to see an useful "Tools Help>Cover Creator" tip sheet. As I say in *How to Get Your Book Published Free in Minutes and Marketed Worldwide in Days*

> Be sure you know what front cover image (and) photo ... you want to use and where they are hiding in your files. You will also want to write enticing back cover copy, or perhaps front cover copy, depending on which of the 33 de-

sign templates you pick. You can go back and edit. Be sure your text color is strong (or dark) enough to be clearly read and that your colors when used together aren't too bizarre.

For Lulu, if I were designing my own cover there, I would follow the directions at the Lulu Cover Wizard. It's well laid out and not very hard to use, but be certain to save at every step or Lulu will erase your progress and send you back to the start! Worse yet, there's nobody at Lulu that you can refer to for help. But it is fun playing with colors and fonts and images, and for a graduation book that hasn't any commercial pretensions, this prefab cover may be fine. When you have it like you want it, hit the "Make a Print-Ready Cover" button, and review it on your computer screen seconds later.

A final thought about the ready-to-go covers. They can only be used with that publisher's books. For example, you can't design a Lulu cover, then use it at CreateSpace (or anywhere else). But if you design your own (or have it designed) and you decide to publish your book at, say, three different publishers, you can use the same basic cover over and over.

In the next chapter, I will include many of the steps you will follow to create a cover at CreateSpace or Lulu or to submit a ready-to-go cover that you or a hired gun will prepare separately and import by file to the publisher.

"The roots of education are bitter, but the fruit is sweet."

Aristotle (384 BC-322 BC)

"The difference between school and life? In school you're taught a lesson and then given a test. In life, you're given a test that teaches you a lesson."

Tom Bodett (1955-   )

Chapter 11

## Submitting the book to the publisher

Once you know the publisher you want to use, the process of submitting the book is straightforward: you need an interior text file and a cover file.

Which means if the book was written as a Word document (or the equivalent on a Mac), it must be saved, for the bound book, in the format the publisher prefers. For both CreateSpace and Lulu, that format is PDF.

So, let's focus here on the bound book process, drawing primarily from *How to Get Your Book Published Free in Minutes and Marketed Worldwide in Days*. Let's start with Amazon's CreateSpace.

### CreateSpace / Bound Books

Assuming you will be doing the submission process yourself, the following 20 steps will help you get your book accepted by CreateSpace and printed almost free—without having to learn much about publishing or having to pay others a bundle for printing (usually hundreds to thousands of dollars) to get Ben's big day remembered in print forever. The folks at CreateSpace are also friendly and helpful. Just email them if you get lost.

1. Open www.createspace.com.

2. The first page says "Publish your words, your way," then gives you two paths to follow. One, open an account immediately. The other, take a look-see at what CreateSpace offers and what it needs from you.

3. Duh. Do the latter, although how to do that isn't obvious. There are three choices at the bottom of the same blue box, below a goldenrod item where it says "Start a title for free." Select "Authors" to enter the world of explanation before you must comply, then find the link "Learn more" above and open it. What appears is an excellent overview of the process.

4. If you want written explanations of the way CreateSpace will work with you to produce your High School Graduation Book, go to any of the items on this Authors page, including Overview, Cover, Interior, Printing Options, Distribution and Royalties, and Buying Copies. Don't be frightened by the new terminology or the necessary steps needed to get your book accepted—it's easier than it looks.

5. Some of the things you will discover are that all book covers are printed in full color and can be done free, you can get a free ISBN (you just saved $225), they will handle all of the orders for you, there is no standing inventory (they produce each book as it's ordered so you needn't invest in printing a starting stock), the agreement with them is non-exclusive, and you will receive a bit of royalty [about 30%] on every bound book sold.

6. At the Interior page, in the "Free Do-It-Yourself Option," click Submission Requirements, where you can find the book sizes that CS offers. (You will probably want 6" x 9," but there are

lots of choices. Whichever you select, your cover must be the same size!) Pick a size and you will see a page template link. That's a blessing. You will simply type your book on that page and the resulting copy will be ready-to-use, properly sized! (That means that the template has the correct margins and layout directions for a header and/or a footer posted.)

7. If you want to hear a first-rate summary of what you just read, find the Self-Publishing Video Overview, right above "Distribution and Royalties." Open the link that asks "Why self-publish your book with us?"

8. Convinced? Now it's time to "Create a New Account." Find that link in the blue banner near the top of any page. Fill it in, then log in.

9. We'll look at the details in a moment, but in a nutshell, you must give your new book a title, like "Ben Barker's High School Graduation Book." Then you provide the needed materials for six major categories: Title Information, Physical Properties, ISBN, Interior,

Cover, and Complete Setup (the last is a checklist of completion of the previous five.)

10. The core of what you send is the Interior (your book's contents in one file) and the Cover (in another file). Later, you will see these combined into a mock version of the final, printed book. If it's acceptable, you will order a proof to be printed and mailed to you (in a few days). That will cost about $25. If that printed book is what you want, you give an OK and the book is ready to be ordered: as Ben's gift, as many copies as you want for the family, or for anybody in the world who wants to join Ben's happy throng.

11. Let's go back and look at (or complete) the paperwork. The five sections in "Title Setup" don't require much explanation from me: Title, Author, Description (very important that it be accurate and concise), Contributors (here you might list your helpers, like the proofreader, photographer(s), illustrator or cover designer, etc.), and a Subtitle (if needed).

12. Remember to save each item and page as you complete it—or you'll have to do it again!

13. "Physical Properties" is where you pick black and white as your book's interior type, the trim size, and the paper color (white unless there's a reason to use cream).

14. What is this mysterious ISBN on the next page? It's an identifying number that all books must have in some format—and it's to be avoided when possible because its cost is pretty much a rip-off. You are the big winner here because CreateSpace will provide you with a free ISBN! Check that box. (You can find out about copyright here too.)

15. Now comes the big stuff without which Ben has no gift! You must provide the guts (copy, photos, anything inside the cover). Then the cover.

16. You have your entire book stored in two files, one of interior book copy, the other, the cover. Both should be in ready-to-go PDF format. In the "Interior" and "Cover" sections is where you

upload each formatted file in its respective box, for submission.

17. Now check the "Complete Setup" to verify that the preceding five sections have been completed. You can't get to the file review section until this is done and accepted.

18. When you click "Submit for Publishing," CS will look it over to see that it meets their submission requirements. In the next day or two they will let you know by e-mail whether it's okay as is or it needs changes. If the latter, they will tell you how to update (change) the files. If it's ready to go, it's time to order your proof! Appropriately, you complete the "Order Proof" and "Print Ready" pages.

19. It takes about a week to receive your printed proof in the mail. Read it closely, and if it's acceptable to give to Ben (and share with your family and the world), tell CreateSpace. If not, send back the corrections. Alas, if you return it, you must buy another proof (which

really means you must pay the shipping again).

20. Then, as the book is being prepped and the proof is being sent to you, look at the Distributor and the Sales and Marketing Categories. At the outset, I wouldn't upgrade to the Pro level, but do insert your book's list price (you set the price and you can change it later), keep the Amazon and eStore sections enabled, mark the e-book boxes at Public and US and international sales, and, for the present, don't upgrade to EDC.

Whew! This being an author and publisher is hard work. You wonder why 99% of your friends' kids will graduate without their own personal High School Graduation Book? But you did it! You are a published author and Ben is one of a million with a lifetime memento of a lifetime accomplishment, thanks to you. Whew again! Giant congratulations!

## Lulu / Bound Books

Another publishing choice for your high school graduation opus is Lulu, which is very large, not the easiest to use, and, of the seven, the least cooperative with assistance—no personal contacts and the robots will usually send you to irrelevant Q & A's.

But what is impressive is the spread of books that Lulu offers in unique layout formats: photo books, calendars, cookbooks, and poetry imprints. It will also take your bound book copy and create an e-book download version without you even being involved.

So here's a summary outline of what you must do to get the Lulu imprint on your graduation book:

1. Open up www.Lulu.com. Or see the small Lulu Demo > link in the middle of the top of the first Web page and watch the short video. When it's done, click the "Publish" button to see the kinds of choices and decisions that are available.

2. Then go to the "Books" box, top left column, hit it, and continue down the

left side of the new page and find "Publishing Tutorials." You only need see "Learn How to Publish a Book" since the second tutorial, about covers, is included in the first. Find the goldenrod link box and push "Start Publishing"—look to the right of the tutorial link.

3. It will now ask you to select the kind of book you want: paperback or hardcover. Tell it paperback for now—open "Make a Paperback Book." Later, check the prices for the hardcover book—you can switch formats when you wish. (The rest of the steps are very similar for both kinds of books.)

4. Again, two choices. The title (you can change it right up to point of creating your proof) and the author (you).

5. Then you are asked how you plan to sell your book through Lulu. I'd pick #2 and use their free ISBN. [Later, you will click the "Get a free ISBN from Lulu.com" button.)

6. On the "Choose Your Project Options" page, select U.S. Trade (6" x 9"), perfect bound printing, and b-w printing with a color cover. Remember that

for Lulu the number of pages in the book must be divisible by four, so add blank pages at the end if needed. (Disregard the book cost chart here. You will get a more reliable cost later.)

7. If you use the free ISBN that Lulu gives you, later you will be told how to list that ISBN info both on your copyright page near the front of your book and how it must appear in the barcode on the back cover. (It may be automatically inserted if you use Lulu's online cover tool.) If you are creating your own cover, just send the barcode to your cover designer.

8. The next page is "Add Files." Here you send Lulu your book's contents. Lulu has lots of clear, helpful links on this page. It wants your work in PDF (so do you, to keep all artwork and images in place), but it will also accept files in .doc, .rtf, and docx, plus images in .jpg, .png, and .gif. If your file is ready, just go to browse, find the book file, and upload it in the box provided. (Be sure you told the PDF converter that the Lulu print pages measure 6" x 9".) Want to see what the file looks like to Lulu? Hit "Take us for a test

drive." If it's not 100% right, go back and change the original file, resave it in PDF, and try it again—and again. If it's accepted, you will see a box (Project Files) saying so on the bottom of this page. If not, it will tell you what must be changed to continue.

9. Lulu is fairly awful about sending you into limbo, to start again, so always hit the SAVE and CONTINUE button at the end of each page, to at least preserve what you've done up to that point!

10. Next page is called "Making Your Print-Ready File." Hit the "Download and Review Your Print-Ready Interior" link. A file will reach you as a separate e-mail, with the book's interior printed out as it would appear in print. It's critical that you get the book exactly as you want it at Step 8 and that it looks as you want it to look here at 10 because soon you will pay for a printed proof. That will take about a week to arrive, and if there still are errors to correct, you must repeat Steps 8 and 10 and pay (and wait) for a second proof. (Each of those proofs costs the printed

price of the book plus shipping.) Save and continue.

11. Cover time! There are two paths here: (1) yours and (2) theirs. The first is where you have completed your own one-piece cover, with front, back, spine, and the ISBN in a bar code, probably all in one PDF file. (Ask the cover creator to send you the .jpg or .gif files, plus the same file saved in PDF.) You may also want to send your designer to the Lulu pages about "Mandatory Requirements for Distribution," the "Book Covers FAQ," and the spine width calculator. Don't panic: most professional cover designers already know the design basics, and if you use the Lulu cover design system, which follows, it is built in. Also, tell the designer to add your ISBN and barcode to your own design: 1.833" x 1" in the bottom right corner of the back cover at least 0.375" from the spine and bottom edge. If the retail price is added, it must match exactly the retail price set (later) for distribution, in US dollars only. Got the file ready? Find the box in the lower left corner of the "Cover Wizard" called "One-Piece Cover Creator" and open it.

It will give the exact dimensions it wants in the PDF. If it's a match, find the file in browse, open it, and tell it to upload. If accepted, the cover appears. Bingo, text and cover ready to go!

12. The alternative is to use the Lulu Cover Wizard. It is kind of a marvel, really. But it also requires lots of fooling around with colors and type size and inserting images—again, remember to save at every step! (If you get lost, go to "My Lulu" and open "My Projects," then activate that book link.)

13. If you decide to use the Cover Wizard, open up the link on the first page of the Cover Wizard where it says "View instructions and info about this step." Hit the + sign to the right to make it easier to read. (You can't print it out but you can bring it up as you progress through the cover-creation steps. To remove it temporarily, hit the "X".) It will walk you through the steps of Changing the Background Cover, Choosing a Theme, Choosing a Layout, Adding Pictures to Your Project Images, Adding Pictures to Your Cover, Adding and Editing the Text, plus Other Tools

and Options: how to save your work, undo and redo buttons, zooming and cropping, and reviewing the cover.

14. The process is shockingly simple, but you must persevere. Note the "back" box lower right. That's to let you roam frontward or backward. Simply do what the drop-down instructions in the previous section say. You can change anything, resize, use different photos, change the theme and background color—just keep previewing to see if this is the kind of book others will consider professional (if that's what you want) or will buy. Making a prefab cover is sort of fun, very limiting, and, of course, Lulu has eager elves waiting to do it for/with you, for pay. When you have precisely what you want, then activate the box on the lower right, "Make a Print-Ready Cover." The cover will be delivered by e-mail in a few minutes.

15. When you save and continue, you are asked to "Describe Your Project." This isn't as important to you as it would be for a commercial book since your book isn't going to be widely bought. So complete the boxes here, in-

sert the language, add the current year and your name in the copyright box, and check "Standard Copyright License."

16. Again, this section is of modest interest since you won't earn much royalty income from the graduation book. Play with the numbers here to see the Lulu print cost, then "Set Your Project Price."

17. You're almost done, with your text and cover posted. If you have changes to make, go backward at "My Projects." Now you wait for the first copy of the book to arrive by mail.

18. When it does, if the book looks just as you want it to, tell Lulu it's accepted. Then buy any copies you want to give others, and tell the rest how it can be ordered from Lulu. You're a published author!

That's how you submit your book and cover to two of the seven ancillary publishers. It must be alarmingly confusing if you're not following these instructions with the webpage tuned in to the page being described.

But let me assure you that it's doable. Proof is that some 400,000 books were printed by Lulu in 2008.

The first time I used these new publishers I invented a book title and went to the websites and just marched through the process (it takes you from page to page) to see how it worked. It was fun and confusing, but it started to make sense right away. Then when I was ready to have them publish a book in truth, it was much easier and faster. If I had the files ready to go, it took from 60-90 minutes on average to do it all.

*Did you know that*

**"High School"**

is used in some parts of the world, particularly in Scotland, North America and Oceania, to describe an institution that provides all or part of secondary education. The term "high school" originated in Scotland with the world's oldest being the Edinburgh's Royal High School, (opened) in 1505. The Royal High School was used as a model for the first public high school in the United States, the English High School founded in Boston, Massachusetts, in 1821. The precise stage of schooling provided by a high school differs from country to country, and may vary within the same jurisdiction.

from *Wikipedia*, the free encyclopedia

**SPECIAL PAGE**

## Possible Additional Costs

The high school graduation book might incur added costs, although most are at your option. How much more might it cost—and why?

* Perhaps nothing if it's an e-book.

* Costs to prepare and mail the final bound book proof ($10-30)

* Proofreading the final copy before submission ($20-100)

* Perhaps some photography expenses (cost of digital camera, photo-related software, and special help getting, sizing, and placing the photos in the interior text)

* Perhaps design and cover prep costs (free to several hundred dollars)

* Possible assistance preparing and posting the interior copy and cover files with the printer

* Conversion of text copy and images if book is prepped as an e-book after being prepared as a bound book ($25-50)

* If the book is a gift for Ben and family members and friends, the cost of the book and shipping (maybe $5-15 a copy, plus shipping)

* _____

* _____

* _____

Chapter 12

## Telling others that the book exists

Assuming that Ben and Betty are regular kids, and so are their families, the public is highly unlikely to clamor to see this graduation book. So setting up some major publicity and promotional campaign is hardly necessary.

Rather, it's enough to tell all of those in the family who appear in the book that it is now available and how they can buy a copy. (Or you might want to buy 12 or 20 at a discount from the publisher and give it to them as your gift.) They can buy the book directly from the publisher you select. The publisher will give you an order link.

Most of the ancillary publishers will help you set up a simple website where you can post all of the ordering information, plus a copy of the cover, the table of contents, some explanatory text about the book, and a few photos with related copy.

You might also ask all of those you contact to share the good news of the book's existence—even more miraculous, that Ben did in fact graduate and here is solid proof! They can send their kin and friends to the website as well.

If you are involved with social networking, Ben's good fortune and the book to prove it will surely be great fodder to share with your followers and contacts. It's a dandy Tweet, good for Facebook, and a nice addition to Linkedin or any other program you are using. In each, you can mention the web link; in most, you can also add some video of the event or a party that follows. Plus a photo or two, and the book cover.

Some families are large and closely bound so you know how far out—how many branches of the tree—you should contact. And you will know who else will be shocked or delighted at Ben's escape and, thus, should at least be informed. That might include other school friends (both yours and Ben's), neighbors, business contacts, bosses where Ben worked, and more.

## Others may want to create their own book

Have you seen other graduation books like yours? Not likely, since the ancillary publishing industry is new and the idea doesn't seem to have caught on—yet!

So you might be on the front crest of a new concept, and others may want a copy of your book as an example of what they can do next year or when their kid graduates. They may want to send a copy to family friends too so they can create their own books. It's even possible that some will want to set up small businesses helping others create graduation books.

So having your book selling through a publisher, plus having a small website giving details and ordering info, could make a lot of sense—and cents. (More when we discuss royalties.)

The ancillary publishers include instructions and some guidance about promoting the books they print, under "marketing."

They are set up to sell the book in digital form almost from the moment you post and approve it. They will list your book in their online digital catalog, and any order that arrives, say from Kindle or iPad customers, will be sold and downloaded in minutes.

More important, several of the ancillary publishers (CreateSpace, PubIt!, and Lulu in particular) are set up to produce P.O.D. (print-on-demand) copies in ink-on-paper bound format as soon as an order arrives from almost any bookstore or distributor, mostly in North America and Europe.

Once you submit a bound copy with a cover to them, they have the files on hand. If you order books, they print what you order and mail them to you in a day or two. They do the same for commercial orders too.

If the unexpected occurs and Ben's graduation book catches buying fire, it is far easier to let the publisher(s) you chose handle the orders (collecting the payment, printing, and shipping) than it is for you to have to establish the mechanism to take orders.

Only when the buying traffic hits 1,000 do you want to think about self-publishing this book. Then look at Lightning Source to create your own starter stock (my book, *How to Get Your Book Published Free in Minutes and Sold Worldwide in Days*, will explain both the ancillary publishing process and how you can expand later into self-publishing).

How could 1,000+ people want to buy this book? By either huge, great, inexplicable good fortune or if Ben gets very famous and there's a demand for memorabilia about him. So make sure the book is accurate and it looks good because folks will all want the original—and then it's too late to make latter-day changes!

"All that stands between the graduate and the top of the ladder is the ladder."

Author Unknown

"Sooner or later we all discover that the important moments in life are not the advertised ones, not the birthdays, the graduations, the weddings, not the great goals achieved. The real milestones are less prepossessing.
They come to the door of memory unannounced, stray dogs that amble in, sniff around a bit and simply never leave. Our lives are measured by these."

Susan B. Anthony (1820-1908)

**SPECIAL PAGE**

## Sample Layout Page

The question is, how can you create a page this size on your computer in which you insert your text and photos? These steps should help create sufficient margins on the top, bottom, and both sides as well as create a uniform layout format for your interior book file:

(1) Go to the File page and open Page Setup
(2) Go to the Paper page and change the Width to 5" and the Height to 8"
(3) Those apply to the Whole document
(4) Go to the Layout page and put an X before the Different odd and even and the Different first page choices. Then the footers will appear where you want them—and not on the Title Page
(5) This layout also applies to the Whole document

(6) Go to the Margins page, select Portrait and Whole document, then enter these numbers for the respective margins: top, 1"; Bottom, 1"; Left, 1", Right, 1"; Gutter, 0", and the Gutter position, Left—or use the CreateSpace layout format.

(7) If you wish to use a footer, open View/Header and Footer and move your mouse to the Footer. Enter a space, type the # key, center the number, and space. If you want a divider line, hit the shift key and type the hyphen to create the line. Center it and space. On the bottom line you enter a title, like Ben Barker's Graduation Book, center it, and close the Header/Footer box.

Chapter 13

## Earning book royalties too

Yes, you will earn royalties on every book sold—except those sold to yourself! But don't start pricing luxury boats yet...

The publisher will tell you the minimum you can charge to get the printing costs covered, and beyond that you can set the book's price. Depending on how they sell the book, your royalty will come from the difference between their charges and your book's price.

Each publisher will suggest a retail price and your royalty rate. As a rough rule, for a bound book you will probably receive royalties from 20-30% of the list price. For the digital version (which never sees paper unless the buyer runs a copy on their home printer), the royalty can be as high as 85%, but is more likely to be 55-70%. The digital price will be lower too. It's often 60-70% of the bound price, but Amazon (Kindle) and Barnes and Noble (PubIt!) pay twice as much (70% royalty) if your list price is from $2.99 to $9.99 than if it's higher or lower.

They pay about 90 days after the sale, and deposit your earnings in your bank account about the first of the month.

Having explained all that, you will most likely earn less than $100 from start to finish. But as I explained in the previous section, lightning may strike and this graduation book could become hotter than a satellite.

What's more important, you have both written (and composed) a book that sort of immortalizes your favorite graduate.

If that's not bad enough, you might have inspired your neighbors or kin, and they in turn might infect their neighbors, friends, and relatives, so scores or hundreds or even millions of otherwise blameless kids can no longer just raise hell, drink beer, and sneak out of high school without it being captured in print and preserved forever.

On the other hand, congratulations! You are at long last profitably in print!

Chapter 14

## Why stop with a graduation book?

Since you're already guilty of sneaking into the literary grove on the back of your kid or grandkid, why not just stick around and write (and publish) more good books?

I know—nobody asked you!

Then consider this both a formal request and blanket permission to use most of the same skills you have honed with your high school graduation book to create as many more books, booklets, reports, white papers, and random folios—things of value in print—as you wish.

The fact that you could have your graduation book quickly and very inexpensively printed by one of the ancillary publishers is just one more proof that there's been a sea change in the publishing world in the 21st century.

No longer must you patiently wait for the big houses to grant you permission to use their printing presses and circulate your book through their distributors. No longer is the commercial value of your book, measured by copies sold, the criterion to seeing print. (In fact, high school graduation books are unlikely to exceed 25-50 sales unless the grad comes from a shamelessly fecund family and you, as the book's author-publisher-hawker, beat the selling drums loud and hard.)

What that means is that the same avenue you just pursued is also there to be taken for all kinds of other books you wish to write—almost any fiction or nonfiction, family history or memoirs, cookbooks (why not those famous fig recipes?), travel, wedding, reunions, business, poetry, photo collections—just look at the library or bookstore shelves and match the topic with your interests, skills, passions, or dreams.

The path is well trod.

Figure out something you simply must put on paper, create a rough outline, and find several other books similar to what you have in mind. Study them to see why and how they work. Then write your own book... Don't edit a word until all the bricks are laid. Then go back and make those bricks sing!

Take a look at the free opening pages of my new book *How to Get Your Book Published Free in Minutes and Marketed Worldwide in Days* if you think it will help.

> See www.gordonburgett.com/ap.htm

Find an ancillary publisher that produces the kind of e- or bound book you want to share, follow their submission path, send the interior and cover files, and in days tell the world that your book exists!

This book describes a model to follow to do two things that are very important: (1) honor a new high school graduate with a book that he or she will cherish, and (2) learn the basic steps that all new writers can use to put their singular ideas and words on paper and in print for the world to see.

In a way, it's your graduation book too. It's your printed admission into the society of writers who change the lives of the world around them.

This special book will also change Ben's life too.

## SPECIAL PAGE

## E-Book? Bound Book? Or both?

We have mentioned the possibility of printing your gift graduation book as a bound book or an e-book—or both. That's rather confusing.

You probably want your book to be as fancy as possible, and to last a long time too. To do that you want a bound book, the kind you see in a bookstore with a front and back cover and a spine.

There are two kinds of e-books. One kind is simply a digital version of the bound book manuscript. If the book is saved as a PDF file, it will look almost the same in either form. Even better, if you can see color in the original text on your computer (in the cover and photos, usually), you can see those same colors in this e-book even though the printed book version may be in black and white. This version is simply the book's files sent as an e-mail attachment or by CD or through some other medium. The recipient can replicate the book on their printer or they can just read it on the monitor. (If you buy the e-book from us, this is the format you receive.)

But when publishers speak of an e-book, they are usually describing the kind of book you can read on a Kindle, Nook, or iPod. To produce those, your book must usually be modified so its contents are free-flowing on a handheld device or a reader. To see a manual that shows how this conversion is done, go to www.smashwords.com. Find the style guide in the lower left column. It's free). This kind of e-book is hard to do for a graduation book because it's hard to make the photos free-flowing.

# Resources: Writing and Publishing

The following books I found the most useful for both writing and publishing books:

* Dan Poynter, *The Self-Publishing Manual* (particularly good on creating your own S-P company)
* John Kremer, *1001 Ways to Sell Your Book* (practical and many paths are free and very effective)
* Pete Masterson, *Book Design and Production* (new, excellent on layout)
* Tom and Marilyn Ross, *The Complete Guide to Self-Publishing* (use the most recent edition)

I particularly enjoy and (l)earn from these websites:

* www.bookmarket.com
* www.parapublishing.com
* www.thebookdesigner.com
* www.ibpa-online.org
* www.spannet.org

I wrote these books because there was nothing that covered the topic adequately (or at all); they are widely recommended by others in the field:

* *How to Get Your Book Published Free in Minutes and Published Worldwide in Days*
* *Niche Publishing: Publish Profitably Every Time*
* *Empire-Building by Writing and Speaking* (just O.P.; some early used copies at Amazon.com)

My blog and my free, monthly newsletter (links below) regularly discuss ancillary publishing, self-publishing, and empire building by writing and speaking.

**blog:**
http://blog.gordonburgett.com
**newsletter:**
http://www.gordonburgett.com/free-reports

*Incidentally, why not tell me when your book is published so I can share that good news with other buyers?*

# INDEX

ancillary publisher, 46,111,113,115,120
barcode, 101,103
Blurb, 61,63,87
bound book, 13,16,20,25,43-6,60-1,63,69, 86, 91,93,99,109-10,119,123,125
camera, 14,16,65-6,70,109
cap, 5-6, 12,28-9,70-2,75,80,112,120
car, 10,15,27,35,39,62,81
ceremony (graduation), 12,17,25-6,28,30, 32,47,56-7,79
checklist,19,25-6,31,39,95
computer, 16,19,32,39,42,66,71-2,82,85, 88,117,125
copyright, 58,69,96,101,106
cover (book), 6,13-4,16,20,23,25,46,59-60, 62,69,77-9,81-9,91,93-6,100-1,103-6, 109,111-2,114,116,119,123,125,128
CreateSpace, 47,60,62-3,87-9,91-3,96-7, 114,116
designer, 54,78,83,87,95,101,103,127
digital, 6-7, 14,20,22,25,44-6,49,56,58,62, 65-6,71,85-6,109,113-4,119,125
diploma, 28,36,70,75-6
distribution (book), 93-4,103
e-book, 6,13,20,25,44,46,61,69,81,84-6, 98-9,109-10,125-6
Facebook, 112,132
footer, 43-5, 94, 117-8
gown, 12,27-9,32,57,75
header, 43, 45, 84, 118
high school graduation book, 5,9,14,44, 50-1,55,58,60,65,79,93-4,98,109,121-2
interior (book), 19-20,29,46,56,62,83,86, 91,93-6,102, 109-10,117,123

iPad, 61,66,104
ISBN, 62,86,93-4,96,100-1,103
JPG, 14,52,66-7,71,101,103
Kindle, 45,61,86,114,119,126
layout, 17,43-4,66,69,75,82-3,94,99, 104, 117-8,124
Lightning Source, 61,86-7,114
Linkedin, 112,132
Lulu, 61, 86-7, 114
PDF, 32,46,53,58,77,84-5,91,96,101-4,125
permission, 31,49-50,52,111,121-2
photo(s), 49,51-4,56-7,65-75,79,81-2,87, 95-6, 99,105,109,112,117
photography, 23,31,109
price (book), 63,83,86,98,100,103,106,119-20
prom, 5,11,26,28,30-2,60,111,113
proof, 7,16,20,32,37,39,47,49,62,76,86,95, 97-8,100,102,107,109,112,121
proofreading, 20,32-3,39,95,109
PubIt, 61,63-4,87,114,119
resources, 22,69,127
royalties, 6-7,60,69,93-4,106,113,119-20
Scribd, 61,86
size (book), 42-4,56,66,69,84-6,93-4,96, 104-5,117
size (photo), 71-3,75
Smashwords, 45,61,86,126
sports, 11,27,39
submission requirements, 93,97
text file, 20,91
timetable, 25,31,39,111
treasure chest, 8,13
Tweet, 112,132
TX form, 58
type font, 43,54
work-for-hire contract, 84

# ORDER FORM

| |
|---|
| **Bound ($15) or Digital ($10) Books** |
| How to Get Your Book Published in Minutes and Marketed Worldwide in Days (2010) |
| Travel Writer's Guide (3rd ed.) |
| Niche Publishing [2008] |
| Your Living Family Tree [2008] |
| How to Plan a Great Second Life (2nd ed.) |
| Treasure and Scavenger Hunts (3rd ed.) |
| **E-Books ($10)** |
| How to Easily and Inexpensively Create Your Own Audio CDs (2009) |
| How to Create an Extraordinarily Effective Speech-Marketing Tool (2010) |
| How To Test Your Niche (Publishing) Market First |
| How to Pick the Right Kind of Publisher (2010) |
| **Audio CD Seminars** |
| (with workbook) |
| How to Sell 75% of Your Travel Writing (2 CDs) |
| How to Set Up and Market Your Own Seminar (2009/4 CDs) |
| How to Create a New, Profitable Publishing Imprint (2010/4 CDs) |
| Actually Writing Query Letters and Articles That Almost Always Sell! |
| How to Test Your Niche (Publishing) Market First (2 CDs) |
| How to Plan a Great Second Life (2010) |

| **Wee e-Books and Reports ($5 or Free)** |
|---|
| 25 Professional Query and Cover Letters |
| Finding Specific Article Topics for Writers |
| 101 Business Tips for Writers and Small Publishers |
| How to Get Your Niche Article in Print 75% of the Time |
| * Lifelong Wealth by Being Indispensable (Free) |
| * 101 Niche Marketing Topics (Free) |
| * Finding Indispensable Article Topics (Free) |

\* with a free newsletter subscription (link below)

For all **details**
(and some **sample chapters)**, see
www.gordonburgett.com/order3.htm

[digital products immediately downloaded]

www.gordonburgett.com
(800) 563-1454
info@glburgett.com

Free monthly newsletter at
http://www.gordonburgett.com/nl.htm

Twitter GLeeBurgett

Blog http://blog.gordonburgett.com
also Facebook + Linkedin

www.ingramcontent.com/pod-product-compliance
Lightning Source LLC
Chambersburg PA
CBHW071308060426
42444CB00034B/1660